Negotiating
Outcomes

Pocket Mentor Series

The *Pocket Mentor* Series offers immediate solutions to common challenges managers face on the job every day. Each book in the series is packed with handy tools, self-tests, and real-life examples to help you identify your strengths and weaknesses and hone critical skills. Whether you're at your desk, in a meeting, or on the road, these portable guides enable you to tackle the daily demands of your work with greater speed, savvy, and effectiveness.

Books in the series:

Leading Teams

Running Meetings

Managing Time

Managing Projects

Coaching People

Giving Feedback

Leading People

Negotiating Outcomes

Writing for Business

Giving Presentations

Negotiating Outcomes

Expert Solutions to Everyday Challenges

Harvard Business School Press

Boston, Massachusetts

No part of this publication may be reproduced, stored in or introduced into a re-trieval system, or transmitted, in any form, or by any means (electronic, mechanical, photocopying, recording, or otherwise), without the prior permission of the pub-lisher. Requests for permission should be directed to permissions@hbsp.harvard.edu, or mailed to Permissions, Harvard Business School Publishing, 60 Harvard Way, Boston, Massachusetts 02163.

Library of Congress Cataloging-in-Publication Data
Negotiating outcomes : expert solutions to everyday challenges.
    p. cm. — (Pocket mentor series)
  Includes bibliographical references.
  ISBN 978-1-4221-1476-6 (pbk. : alk. paper)
  1. Negotiation in business. I. Harvard Business School Publishing
Corporation.
  HD58.6.N335 2007
  658.4'052—dc22

                          2007000876

The paper used in this publication meets the requirements of the American National Standard for Permanence of Paper for Publications and Documents in Libraries and Archives Z39.48-1992

Contents

Four Key Concepts   15

Understanding these key concepts will put you in a good position the next time you negotiate.

Nine Steps to a Deal   23

If you follow these nine steps, you will be prepared to make the most of any negotiation.

Negotiation Tactics 37

Once you get to the negotiation table, you must select and implement tactics that will help you achieve your objectives.

Barriers to Agreement   51

The human foibles of pride, impatience, stubbornness, or ignorance of the facts can come between negotiators and a deal. You must understand the typical barriers to agreement and know how to overcome them.

Cognitive Traps   57

Negotiating has one thing in common with tennis: the winner is often the one who makes the fewest mistakes. Once you understand the main types of cognitive traps, you'll be prepared to avoid them.

The Skills of Effective Negotiators   65

What makes an effective negotiator? This section describes skills you can learn and sharpen with practice.

Tips and Tools   71

Tools for Negotiating Outcomes   73

Worksheets you can use to guide your preparations and negotiating sessions.

Test Yourself   79

A helpful review of concepts presented in this guide. Take it before and after you've read the guide to see how much you've learned.

Frequently Asked Questions   85

Look here for answers and practical advice on overcoming typical negotiating problems.

Key Terms   91

Every discipline has a special vocabulary. The art of negotiating is no different. Read this list to learn the language of negotiators.

To Learn More   95

Articles and books that can help you further master this topic.

Sources for Negotiating Outcomes   101

Notes   103

Use this Notes section to record your ideas.

Mentor's Message: Negotiating Skills Will Help Your Career

If you are a supervisor, manager, or executive, you probably spend a good part of your day negotiating with people inside or outside your organization. These negotiations may be formal meetings across a bargaining table, or they may be informal exchanges between you and your employees. In both cases, proficient and refined negotiating skills are required for success.

This Pocket Mentor explains the negotiating process and teaches you how to become an effective practitioner. It will help you to

- Understand the basic types of negotiation and the key concepts underlying them

- Prepare for, conduct, and close a negotiation

- Maintain a good negotiating relationship with the other side and maximize value for both sides

- Avoid common errors and overcome common barriers to agreement

Marjorie Corman Aaron, Mentor

Marjorie Corman Aaron, JD, is a mediator, trainer, and professor with more than eighteen years' experience in mediation, negotiation, and dispute resolution. She spent four years as executive director of the renowned Program on Negotiation at Harvard Law School, from which was born the best-selling book *Getting to Yes* by Roger Fisher, William Ury, and Bruce Patton. Dr. Aaron is currently a professor of practice and the director of the Center for Practice in Negotiation and Problem Solving at the University of Cincinnati College of Law, where she teaches negotiation and dispute resolution. She uses an in-depth understanding of the theory of negotiation as well as her practical experience of having mediated hundreds of business and legal disputes to help managers and students develop the skills and judgment to be better negotiators. In addition, she was a contributing writer on this book.

Negotiating Outcomes: The Basics

Types of
Negotiations

Let us never negotiate out of fear,
but let us never fear to negotiate.
—John F. Kennedy

NEGOTIATION IS THE PROCESS by which people deal with their differences. Whether those differences involve the purchase of a new automobile, a labor contract dispute, the terms of a sale, or a complex alliance between companies, resolutions are typically sought through negotiations. To negotiate is to seek mutual agreement through dialogue.

There are two kinds of negotiation: *distributive negotiation* and *integrative negotiation.* Most negotiations combine elements of both types, but for the purposes of understanding, it's important to examine each type in its pure form.

Distributive negotiation

In a distributive negotiation, parties compete over the distribution of a fixed sum of value. The key question in a distributed negotiation is, "Who will claim the most value?" A gain by one side is made at the expense of the other. This is also known as a *zero-sum* negotiation.

Examples of distributive negotiations include the following:

- **The sale of a car.** There is no relationship between the buyer and the seller, and all that matters is the price. Each side works for the best deal, and any gain by one party represents a loss to the other.

- **Negotiations over the price of real estate.** The sellers know that any amount conceded to the buyer will come out of their own pockets, and vice versa.

Often, there is only one issue in a distributive negotiation: money. The seller's goal is to negotiate as high a price as possible; the buyer's goal is to negotiate as low a price as possible. A dollar or euro more to one side is a dollar or euro less to the other. Thus, the seller and the buyer compete to claim the best deal possible for themselves, and the bottom line defines what is possible.

In a distributive negotiation, it is impossible to make trade-offs based on differing preferences. Because there is only one issue at stake, you can't trade more of what is highly valued by one party against a different item or issue highly valued by the other party. Thus, the deal is confined: there are no opportunities for creativity or for enlarging the scope of the negotiation.

Similarly, relationship and reputation are irrelevant; the negotiators are not willing to trade value in the deal for value in their relationship with the other negotiator.

Integrative negotiation

The second kind of negotiation is integrative negotiation. In this type of negotiation, parties cooperate to achieve maximum benefits by integrating their interests into an agreement. This is also known as a *win-win* negotiation.

In business, integrative negotiations tend to occur at these times:

- During the structuring of complex, long-term partnerships or other collaborations

- When the deal involves many financial and nonfinancial terms

- Between professional colleagues or superiors and direct subordinates whose long-term interests benefit from the other's satisfaction

In an integrative negotiation, there are many items and issues to be negotiated, and the goal of each side is to "create" as much value as possible for itself and the other side. Each side makes trade-offs to get the things it values most, giving up other, less critical factors.

When parties' interests differ, your ability to claim what you want from the deal does not necessarily detract from the other party's ability to claim what it wants. Both parties' interests and preferences may be satisfied. Consider this example:

> *Harvey and his neighbor, Steve, have talked off and on about their sailboats. Harvey has a 33-foot sloop with a nicely outfitted cabin and inboard motor—a great vessel for coastal cruising. Steve wants to own it if Harvey will*

come up with a price Steve can afford. And although Harvey has never mentioned it to his neighbor, he secretly admires Steve's 25-foot boat. It is small and has fewer amenities, but, as Harvey tells himself, "Heck, I don't enjoy taking care of a big boat any more. Sometimes a small boat is more fun to sail."

As they talk further, Harvey realizes that he has something that his neighbor values more highly than he does. And Steve sees it the same way. Given this situation, they can negotiate a boat trade in which each will realize value while giving up something that he values much less.

Finding opportunities for mutual benefit requires cooperation and disclosure of information. Each party needs to understand its own key interests and the key interests of the other side.

Distributive versus integrative negotiations

Characteristic	Distributive	Integrative
Outcome	Win-lose	Win-win
Motivation	Individual gain	Joint and individual gain
Interests	Opposed	Different but not always opposite
Relationship	Short-term	Long-term or short-term
Issues involved	Single	Multiple
Ability to make trade-offs	Not flexible	Flexible
Solution	Not creative	Creative

The negotiator's dilemma

Most business negotiations are neither purely distributive nor purely integrative; rather, competitive and cooperative elements are intertwined. The resulting tension, known as the *negotiator's dilemma,* requires difficult strategic choices. Negotiators must balance competitive strategies, which make it hard to cooperate and create value effectively, with cooperative strategies, which make it hard to compete and claim value effectively. At the core of the negotiator's art is knowing whether to compete where interests conflict—claiming more instead of less—or to create value by exchanging the information that leads to mutually advantageous options.

Multiphase and Multiparty Negotiations

M OST PEOPLE ENVISION A negotiation as two people or teams sitting opposite each other at the bargaining table; the individual parties eventually come to an agreement or walk away. This characterization is fairly accurate for one-on-one negotiations that can be handled in a single meeting, such as the purchase of a car or a discussion between a supervisor and a subordinate about job performance and wages.

Few negotiations are so simple. Most involve more than two parties, and they sometimes take place in phases, with each phase devoted to unique issues.

Multiphase negotiations

Multiphase transactions are negotiations implemented over time in different phases. As parties proceed through the phases, each upholding its respective promises, future dealings ensue. The context of multiphase negotiations allows parties to negotiate based on follow-through and continuing communication.

Here are examples of multiphase negotiations:

- The buyout of an inventory-based business in which the parties set a price for the business and then agree to modify it later based on the value of the inventory on a specific date

- An architectural design contract in which the architect and client agree on a price for the design phase of a project and then use the design to agree on a price for the completion of construction drawings

You can do certain things during the early and final phases of a multiphase negotiation that will help you achieve success. During the early phases, remember these tips:

- Become familiar with the other party's communication and negotiation style. This knowledge will help you be more effective in the later, more critical phases.

- Build trust. Follow through on all agreements and promises so that the other party sees that you are trustworthy and cooperative.

- Monitor the other party to ensure that it is following through on agreements and promises. A party's failure to perform as promised in an early phase is a warning signal of the need to create enforcement mechanisms, security provisions, or other sanctions against future nonperformance.

- Walk away from disconcerting negotiations. If the other party intentionally fails to follow through on agreements or promises, end the negotiations while you still can.

During the final phases, remember these guidelines:

- Ensure that the final phase is not the most significant in money or impact, nor the most difficult. This practice will help protect you when incentives to breach are the greatest. Most parties will not risk great injury to reputation by failing to perform an insignificant item.

- Pay attention to early warnings. Create enforcement mechanisms against nonperformance or other breaches of trust when the other party's promises have not been upheld.

Multiparty negotiations

Business and professional negotiations commonly involve more than two parties, and generally more than two people. In multiparty negotiations, coalitions or alliances can form among the parties and influence the process and outcome. Coalitions have more power than any individual party involved in the negotiation.

There are at least two types of coalitions:

- **Natural coalitions.** These form between allies that share a broad range of common interests. For example, an environmental agency and a citizen's nature conservation group share basic agendas and will often work in concert to block development initiatives, even without an explicit agreement to do so.

- **Single-issue coalitions.** These form when parties that differ on other issues unite to support or block a single issue, often for different reasons. For example, a labor union and a nature conservation group might form a coalition to block an anti-union developer from building a shopping mall in a wooded area. Each group has a different reason for joining the coalition.

To be successful in multiparty negotiations, you must determine your party's interests and goals at the negotiation table, as well as those of the coalitions you're dealing with, and then form a strategy. If your party is relatively weak, consider forming a coalition with others to improve your bargaining power. If your party is up against a coalition, you might find ways to break apart the coalition.

A natural coalition is hard to break, because the parties are closely aligned; a single-issue coalition, however, is more vulnerable. Because the parties involved in a single-issue coalition have different reasons for joining, it is often possible to address the demands of one party, leaving the other party standing on its own. For example, if a labor union and a nature conservation group form a coalition to block an anti-union developer from building a shopping mall, the property owner might find a different developer with a better track record in dealing with unions. As a result, the union might be more likely to withdraw its opposition, leaving the conservationists to fight alone.

No matter which type of negotiation you're faced with, it's bound to be complex if it involves multiple phases or multiple parties. In both cases, you need to be proactive about protecting your interests. In multiphase negotiations, use the early phases to evaluate the other party and build trust, and structure the later phases so that they are difficult to breach. In multiparty negotiations, consider the benefits of either forming or breaking coalitions to improve your bargaining power.

NOTE: A coalition is a temporary alliance of separate entities or individuals who join together to seek a common purpose. A coalition can strengthen your negotiating position. Coalition-building can also extend a manager's influence within an organization.

Four Key Concepts

W HEN PEOPLE DON'T have the power to force a certain outcome or behavior, they negotiate—but only when they believe it is to their advantage. A negotiated solution is advantageous only when a better option is not available. Therefore, any successful negotiation must have a fundamental framework based on knowledge of three things:

- The best alternative to a negotiation

- The minimum threshold for a negotiated deal

- How flexible a party is willing to be and what trade-offs it is willing to make

Four concepts are especially important for establishing this framework.

- **BATNA (best alternative to a negotiated agreement):** your options if you fail to reach agreement during a negotiation. (Note: This term was first used by Roger Fisher and William Ury of the Harvard Program on Negotiation in their famous book, *Getting to Yes.*)

- **Reservation price:** the least favorable point at which you'll accept a negotiated deal; the "walk-away" price.

- **ZOPA (zone of possible agreement):** the range in which a potential deal can take place; defined by the overlap between the parties' reservation prices.

- **Value creation through trades:** the trading of goods or services that have only modest value to their holders but exceptional value to the other party.

BATNA: The best alternative to a negotiated agreement

Your BATNA is your preferred course of action in the absence of a deal. Knowing your BATNA means knowing what you'll do or what will happen if you do not reach agreement.

For example, suppose a consultant is negotiating with a potential client about a month-long assignment. It's not clear what fee arrangement she'll be able to negotiate, or even whether she'll reach an agreement. Before she meets with the potential client, she determines her best alternative to a negotiated agreement—her BATNA. In this case, her BATNA is to spend that month developing marketing materials for other clients—work she estimates she can bill at $15,000. When she meets with the potential client, her goal is to reach an agreement that will yield her at least $15,000, and preferably more.

Your BATNA determines the point at which you can say no to an unfavorable proposal; thus, it is critical to know your BATNA before entering into any negotiation. If you don't, you won't know

A Caution on BATNA Values

Although it's essential that you know your own BATNA and try to estimate that of the other side, be aware that most people don't do a good job
of estimating BATNA values. One team of scholars describes an experi-
ment involving the value of a company for sale. "Even given identical business information, balance sheets, income statements, and the like," they
write, "those assigned to buy the company typically rate its true value as
low, while those assigned to sell it give much higher best estimates. Neutral observers tend to rank the potential somewhere in between."

The lesson here is that BATNA values can be influenced by your personal perspective. So be as objective as possible. Check your thinking
with a neutral third party.

Source: David A. Lax and James K. Sebenius, *The Manager as Negotiator* (New York: Free Press, 1986), 57–58.

whether a deal makes sense or when to walk away. You might reject
a good offer that is much better than your alternative, or you
might accept a weak offer, one that is less favorable than what you
could have obtained elsewhere if there was no agreement.

The reservation price

Your reservation price, also referred to as your walk-away, is the
least favorable point at which you would accept a deal. Your reservation price should be derived from your BATNA but is not necessarily the same thing. Your reservation price and BATNA will be

similar if the deal is only about money and if a credible monetary offer is your BATNA.

For example, when preparing to negotiate with a commercial landlord over a lease for office space, you consider that you are currently paying $20 per square foot. This number is your BATNA. You also take into account that the new location would be closer to clients and would provide a more attractive workspace, and thus you'd be willing to pay $30 per square foot. That's your reservation price. If more than $30 per square foot is required, you'll walk away and attempt to lease space in a different building. During the negotiation the landlord insists on $35 per square foot and won't accept anything lower, thereby indicating that his reservation price is $35 per square foot.

You can use the worksheet "Determining Your Reservation Price" to guide your calculations.

NOTE: Your reservation price is just as important as your BATNA. So give its formulation equal attention. Together, a solid reservation price and BATNA will give you the confidence you need to negotiate your deal.

ZOPA: The zone of possible agreement

The ZOPA is the range in which a deal can take place. Each party's reservation price determines one end of the ZOPA. The ZOPA itself exists, if at all, in the overlap between these high and low limits, that is, between the parties' reservation prices.

Determining Your Reservation Price

Use this worksheet to examine the variables that can determine your reservation price.

1. Explore the variables that affect your reservation, or "walk-away," position.

What is the value to you of the deal on the table?

How does this compare to the value of your BATNA?

What other values need to be considered?

If there is a dollar number involved in the negotiation, what is the lowest amount that you would consider?

What are the minimum nondollar terms that you would consider?

2. Evaluate the trade-offs between your issues and interests.

Which issues or terms do you care most about?

Are any of these issues or terms linked? *(That is, does more or less of what you want on one issue give you more or less flexibility on any of the others?)*

How much of what you want on one issue or term would you trade off against another?

Are there different package deals that would be equivalent in value to you?

3. Articulate the parameters of your reservation price. *(The resulting terms or price create the context for you to evaluate alternative proposals.)*

Zone of possible agreement

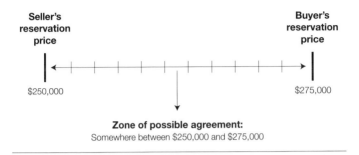

Zone of possible agreement:
Somewhere between $250,000 and $275,000

Consider this example. A buyer has set a reservation price of $275,000 for the purchase of a commercial warehouse and would like to pay as little as possible. The seller has set a reservation price of $250,000 and would like to obtain as much as possible. The ZOPA, therefore, is the range between $250,000 and $275,000.

If the numbers were reversed—if the buyer had set a reservation price of $250,000 and the seller had set a reservation price of $275,000—there would be no ZOPA, no overlap in the range in which they would agree. No agreement would be possible, no matter how skilled the negotiators, unless there were other elements of value to be considered—or one or both sides' reservation prices changed.

Value creation through trades

Another key concept of negotiation is value creation through trades, the idea that negotiating parties can improve their positions by trading the values at their disposal. Value creation through trades occurs in the context of integrated negotiations. Each party usually gets something it wants in return for something it values much less.

For example, suppose that Helen and John, two collectors of rare books, are entering a negotiation. Helen is interested in purchasing a first-edition Hemingway novel from John to complete her collection. During their negotiation, John mentions that he is looking for a specific William Prescott book, which Helen happens to own and is willing to part with. In the end, John sells Helen the Hemingway book, completing her collection, for $100 plus her copy of the Prescott book. Both parties are satisfied. The goods exchanged have only modest value to their original holders, but exceptional value to their new owners.

Nine Steps
to a Deal

E VERY IMPORTANT ENDEAVOR benefits from preparation. Negotiating is no different. People who know what they want, what they are willing to settle for, and what the other side is all about stand a better chance of negotiating a favorable deal for themselves. You are more likely to be an effective negotiator if you follow these nine preparatory steps.

Step 1: Determine satisfactory outcomes

A negotiation's success is judged by its outcome; thus, it's best to be clear about what constitutes a good outcome for you and for the other side before the negotiation begins. Satisfactory outcomes typically address the interests—the underlying motivations, concerns, and needs—of each party. Determining the interests of the other side, however, can be difficult—especially in distributive negotiations, in which the negotiating parties tend to conceal their interests. Try to uncover interests by asking questions that can help you ascertain the other party's priorities, concerns, and perspective.

The worksheet "Assessing the Other Side's Interests" is useful for this task.

Assessing the Other Side's Interests

Use this worksheet to summarize your knowledge of the other side's interests. Refer to this information throughout the negotiation process, and use it to identify value-creating opportunities.

Learn about the other side.	Yes	No
1. Have you spoken with people—either formally or informally—who know the other party?		
2. Have you reviewed the other side's Web site, marketing materials, and (if applicable) annual reports and public findings?		
3. Have you researched the other side's industry and contacted sources within the industry to find out more?		
4. Have you imagined what the other side's interests, preferences, and needs would be if you were in its position?		

Assess the other side's BATNA.

What do you know about the other side's business circumstances?
How strong is its financial performance?

What is its strategy?

What are its key corporate initiatives?

What competitive pressures does it face?

What do you know about the value this deal has to the other side?
How important is this deal to the other side at this time?

Is it necessary for the other side to meet a larger objective? *(Describe the objective.)*

What do you know about the availability of a replacement deal?
Is your offer easy to find elsewhere?

Can it be obtained in time to meet the other side's deadlines?

Has the other side already obtained bids from or initiated informal negotiations with anyone else?

Consider the terms the other side would like to see for the deal.

What broader business objectives would the other side like to see served by this deal?

What terms of this deal could hamper its business growth?

What terms might you offer that would benefit the other side (at a low cost to you)?

What Would YOU Do?

How Much Is Too Much?

W HEN A LICE STARTED recruiting Manuel, she knew
he'd provide the expertise the department needed—
and she knew he'd be expensive. But now his demands seem to be
escalating out of control. So far, Alice has upped the already high
salary, added extra vacation time, and increased the number of his
stock options. Now Manuel is asking for an extra performance-
based bonus. Alice reviews the list of other candidates. The clos-
est qualified applicant is very eager for the job but lacks the
experience that Manuel would bring. Alice prefers Manuel, but
she is uncomfortable with his increasing demands. Should she say
no on principle, and risk losing him? Or should she agree to his lat-
est request and hope it is the last? What would you do?

Step 2: Identify opportunities to create value

Once you understand what a good outcome would look like for
you and the other party, you can identify areas of common
ground, compromise, and opportunities for favorable trades.

Consider the example of Diane, a prized employee who requests an extended leave of absence so that she can be more avail-

able to her child. Her supervisor is concerned that the work in Diane's unit won't be completed in her absence. After uncovering interests and desirable outcomes, they are able to negotiate a mutually satisfying solution. Rather than take an extended leave, Diane agrees to work reduced hours from home. The supervisor is willing to trade her presence on site for completed work, and Diane is willing to trade her extended leave for reduced hours.

Step 3: Identify your BATNA and reservation price

It's critical to know your BATNA and reservation price before a negotiation. It's also prudent to estimate the other party's BATNA and reservation price. If you know this information ahead of time, you'll be able to recognize when you've reached a favorable deal, and you'll have a better sense of when to hold firm or make concessions.

NOTE: Never accept a deal that is worse than your BATNA. In determining your BATNA, however, be sure to account for all the factors involved—even some of the intangible and hard-to-measure ones, such as relationship value.

Step 4: Improve your BATNA

Your BATNA determines the point at which you can say no to an unfavorable proposal. If you have a strong BATNA, you can afford to negotiate for more favorable terms. Therefore, it's wise to try to improve your BATNA before and during deliberations with the other party. For example, you might look for new clients or vendors or try to arrange better agreements with current clients or vendors.

The worksheet "Identifying and Improving Your BATNA" is useful for this task.

Steps for Improving Your Negotiating Position

1. **Improve your BATNA.** A strong BATNA gives you bargaining power. If your BATNA is weak, do what you can to improve it. Depending on your situation, this may involve finding other clients, buyers, vendors, or job offers. Anything that strengthens your BATNA improves your negotiating position.

2. **Identify the other side's BATNA.** This knowledge is another source of negotiation strength. The opposing negotiators won't tell you their BATNA unless it is very strong. They may even bluff about it. Sometimes, however, you can discover the other party's BATNA and circumstances by using the following methods:
   - Contact sources within the industry.
   - Check potentially relevant business publications.
   - Review annual reports (or public filings).
   - Ask questions informally of the negotiators or others within the company.
   - Ask questions during the formal negotiation.
   - Imagine what your interests, preferences, and needs would be if you were in the other side's position.

3. **Weaken the other party's BATNA.** Anything that weakens the other side's BATNA will improve your relative position.

Identifying and Improving Your BATNA

*Use this worksheet to identify and improve your best alternative
to a negotiated agreement, or BATNA.*

1. What are your alternatives to a negotiated agreement?
Make a list of what your alternatives will be if the negotiation ends without agreement.

1.

2.

3.

4.

5.

2. Of the alternatives that you listed, which is your best alternative?

3. Can you improve your BATNA?

Are there any arrangements you can make with other suppliers, partners, or customers that would improve your BATNA?

Are there ways to remove or alter any constraints that currently weaken your BATNA? If yes, what? How?

Are there ways to change your terms of the negotiation to improve your BATNA? If yes, what? How?

4. What will your new BATNA be if you succeed in improving it?

How Needy Are You?

Author and consultant Jim Camp urges his readers to avoid appearing "needy," the equivalent to having a weak BATNA. Shrewd bargainers will take advantage of neediness. Tough negotiators will do whatever they can to encourage neediness in their opponents:

> Tough negotiators are experts at recognizing this neediness in their adversaries, and expert in creating it as well. Negotiators with giant corporations, in particular, will heighten the expectations of their supplier adversaries, painting rosy, exaggerated scenarios for mega-orders, joint ventures, global alliances, all for the purpose of building neediness on the part of their adversary . . . Then, when the neediness is well-established, they lower the boom with changes, exceptions, and . . . demands for concessions.

You can avoid appearing needy by building a strong BATNA and letting the other side know that you are prepared to walk away if it demands too many concessions.

Source: Jim Camp, *Start With No* (New York: Crown, 2002), 4–6.

Step 5: Determine who has authority

It's best to negotiate directly with the person who has the authority to make a decision. Doing so reduces opportunities for misunderstanding and prevents you from proceeding down a path with an unrealistic outcome. Do whatever you can to identify the real decision maker. It's perfectly acceptable to ask about who will be making the decision and to inquire about the decision-making process.

If you cannot negotiate directly with the decision maker, determine the level of authority of the person with whom you will be negotiating so that you can plan accordingly. Sometimes dealing with negotiators who lack full authority has advantages. For example, they may be freer to discuss their company's interests and explore more creative options.

You can use the worksheet "Evaluating Your Authority and That of the Other Side" for this task.

Step 6: Study the other side

Negotiation is a highly interpersonal activity. Therefore, it's advantageous to learn about the personality, style, and background of the people you'll be negotiating with as well as the culture, goals, and values of the organization they represent.

This knowledge can help you form invaluable personal connections and avoid misunderstandings or errors. Find out what you can about the other side by asking questions, talking with people who know the other party, and researching relevant Web sites, annual reports, and marketing materials.

NOTE: Whether you aim for a win-win deal or a zero-sum outcome, understanding the person on the other side of the table will improve your chances of achieving your goal. Is that person a take-no-prisoners negotiator, or a passive operator? How has he performed in previous negotiations? What are his strengths, weaknesses, and interests? As in sports and in war, anything you can do to better understand the other side will put you in a better position.

Evaluating Your Authority and That of the Other Side

Use this worksheet to determine and confirm the authority level you have and the authority level of the persons with whom you will be negotiating, so that you can plan accordingly.

The other side's authority. *(Learn as much as possible about the individuals on the other side.)*

1. Who will be at the negotiating table?

2. What are the formal titles and areas of responsibility of the persons with whom you will be negotiating?

3. How long have they been with the company? What other relevant experience do they have?

4. How is the company structured? *(Is it hierarchical, with significant decision-making powers centered at the top, or is it relatively decentralized?)*

5. How are the negotiators viewed within the organization? *(Are they generally respected, listened to, etc.? Rely on contacts outside the organization, if available.)*

6. What are their other interests outside work (e.g., sports, hobbies, volunteer interests, political orientation, children)?

Your authority. *(Confirm in as much detail as possible.)*

What kind of deal are you authorized to make? (Complete as appropriate.)

Only a predetermined deal for which committee approval has been obtained? *(If yes, describe. If you can also negotiate something "better" beyond the predetermined deal, what does the committee consider "better"?)*

Only a deal that meets certain objectives? *(What are the objectives? Do you have the freedom to structure the deal in the best way you can?)*

Would the committee prefer that you bring a deal back for formal review and approval?

Is your authority limited on monetary issues but not on other creative options without significant financial implications?

Are you authorized to provide information about your company's needs, interests, and preferences if the other side engages in a good-faith, reciprocal exchange?

Step 7: Prepare for flexibility in the process

Negotiations don't always follow a predictable or linear path. Relationships may become unpleasant, or a negotiator may be replaced. Unanticipated developments can cause the other side to delay the process. Newly found opportunities may encourage the other side to drive a harder bargain.

To overcome these roadblocks, you need to be flexible and patient. Don't assume that the negotiation must proceed according to a predetermined course. Be prepared to deal with new people and unanticipated developments. Rather than seeing each change in the process as a problem, try to treat change as an opportunity for learning and creativity.

NOTE: Managers are action-oriented people. They want to move things along quickly to desired conclusions. That's a useful trait in most aspects of organizational life, but it doesn't always serve managers well during difficult negotiations, which demand patience.

Step 8: Gather objective criteria to establish fairness

In any negotiation, both sides want to believe that any deal reached is fair and reasonable. This is especially important when the parties expect to have a continuing relationship. To establish what is fair and reasonable, you can use external, objective criteria. For example, you might research current and comparable market values of properties before establishing a price for your land or before making someone an offer.

Because there may be many relevant criteria for fairness and reasonableness, it's important to research which criteria might be applied to your situation. Be prepared to explain why criteria that are more favorable to you are more relevant, and why criteria that are less favorable to you are less relevant. If you can convince the other side that a certain criterion or formula is fair and reasonable, the other party will find it harder to reject a proposal incorporating the standard and will more likely feel satisfied with the final deal.

Step 9: Alter the process in your favor

If, during a negotiation, you start to feel that your ideas are being ignored or that the meetings are rigged to produce a particular result, heed those feelings. It's likely that whoever set the agenda did so with a particular outcome in mind, or that participants are deferring to someone with greater organizational clout. Or your ideas may be out of step with those of others.

This type of situation warrants a change in the process. This doesn't mean that you should try to change the substantive *issues* being discussed. Rather, you should address logistical factors such as where the meeting occurs, who attends, and the sequence of the agenda. These elements can influence the way others participate and react in meetings.

You can also work behind the scenes to educate others about your ideas. Talk with people who are respected and influential, and form a coalition. You might also reposition the issue being discussed so that others consider it from a different perspective.

What You COULD Do.

Set Your Limit.

Alice needs to determine her best alternative to a negotiated agreement. Knowing her BATNA means knowing what she will do or what will happen if she does not reach agreement in the negotiation at hand. For example, Alice should set clear limits on what she's willing to offer Manuel and analyze the consequences if Manuel turns her down. Would she really be happy hiring a different candidate, or is it worth upping the ante for Manuel?

After she has determined her BATNA, she should then figure out her reservation price—her walk-away number. What is the most she's willing to pay Manuel to join her team? Once she knows her BATNA and reservation price, she should use those as her thresholds in her negotiations and not be swayed by Manuel's demands.

Negotiation
Tactics

Never cut what you can untie.
—Joseph Joubert

WHEN YOU SIT AT THE negotiation table, you face many difficult decisions. Who should make the first offer? What is the best way to frame your offer? Should you hold firm or make concessions? These kinds of decisions are judgment calls, but there are tactics you can use to make the negotiation process go more smoothly and in your favor.

Tactics for getting off to a good start

- **Set a positive tone with your opening remarks.** Express respect for the other side's experience and expertise. Frame the negotiation as a joint endeavor, and emphasize your openness to the other side's interests and concerns.

- **Review the agenda.** This will help ensure that everyone agrees on the issues to be covered. Use this opportunity to make sure that all the parties have a common understanding of the issues to be discussed.

- **Discuss your expectations regarding process.** People often have different assumptions about how the negotiation

should work. Some expect proposals to be made at the out-
set, but others expect an open discussion of the issues first.
Listen carefully to this discussion of the process; it will tell
you a great deal about the other side's negotiating style.

- **Offer information.** Voluntarily explain some of your interests
and concerns first as a good-faith measure. If the other side
does not reciprocate, however, be cautious about providing
additional information.

Tips for Establishing the Right Tone

- Don't overlook the importance of casual conversation at the begin-
ning of the negotiation. It helps make everyone feel less defensive,
and more cooperative and communicative.

- Even in a distributive negotiation, casual conversation helps you
get to know the other side better. It makes you better able to judge
when the other negotiator is being truthful.

- Take your cue from what the casual conversation reveals about the
other negotiator's style and manner.

- If the other side is more formal, don't speak too casually. Doing so
might be interpreted as a lack of seriousness on your part.

- If the other side is informal, speak in a more casual way.

Tactics for distributive negotiations

In most distributive negotiations, a gain by one side represents a loss to the other side. You can use several techniques to achieve gains and prevent losses.

- **Do not disclose any significant information about your circumstances.** It is best if you do not reveal why you want to make a deal, your real interests or business constraints, your preferences among issues or options, or the point at which you'd walk away. It is advantageous to let the other side know that you have options if the deal falls through.

- **Learn as much as possible about the other side.** Investigate why it wants to make a deal, its real interests and business constraints, and its preferences among issues or options.

- **Establish an anchor.** The first offer often sets the bargaining range. Studies show that negotiation outcomes often correlate to the first offer, so start at the right place. It's best to anchor when you have a strong sense of the other side's reservation price; your proposal should be at or just a bit higher than that number. Don't be too aggressive or greedy, or else the other side may walk away. Always be prepared to articulate why your offer is justifiable.

     Note: if you later discover that your anchor point is beyond the range of the other negotiator's price, you will have to retreat gracefully. In this case, make sure that you don't indicate that your initial offer is final. And have a different line of reasoning ready to support your shift to a less aggressive offer.

- **Divert the discussion away from unacceptable anchors.** If the other negotiator makes the first offer, you should recognize and resist its potential power as a psychological anchor. Don't let it set the bargaining range unless you think it's a sensible starting point. If you think the attempted anchor suggests an unfavorable or unacceptable bargaining range, steer the conversation away from numbers and proposals. Focus instead on interests and concerns. Ask questions that focus on the interests and motivations underlying the other side's position. Such questions might reveal new information that can help you reposition your proposal.

  After some time has passed, put *your* initial number or proposal on the table, supported by sound reasoning. To the extent possible, avoid direct comparison between the two offers. If the other party's initial offer was not serious and you ignore it, the other side may also. If it was serious and if the other negotiators refer to it again, you should respectfully ask them to explain why their offer is reasonable.

- **Make cautious concessionary moves.** In a traditional, back-and-forth negotiation over numbers, a large movement signals significant additional flexibility, whereas a very small movement signals that the negotiator is approaching the reservation price. At this point, people tend to move in increasingly small increments, and the other side often expects such a pattern of behavior.

You don't have to follow these conventions, but you do have to understand them; your offers and counteroffers may be interpreted in this light. So if you make a substantial move but are not prepared to move much further, you should say so. Also, be prepared to explain the reason you are willing to make this significant concession—and expect to have your explanation tested by the other side.

- **Use time as a negotiation tool.** Attach an expiration date to any offer to buy. Otherwise, the seller may put you off and wait for a better offer.

- **Offer multiple proposals, and consider packaging options.** Offer at least two proposals, and package options when possible. For example, you might offer $18,000 for a boat and trailer as a package, or $16,000 for the boat alone. With options, the other party won't feel stuck with an ultimatum. Also, the other party may compare the proposals to each other instead of to the original goals, and that can work to your advantage.

- **Tap into, but don't be trapped by, the power of fairness and legitimacy.** No one likes being exploited. Deals often fall apart when one side is convinced it is being fair while the other side is not. What seems fair to you is determined largely by your perspective. If the other side asserts a position you believe to be unfair, ask, "What makes you believe your position is fair?" Then, after expressing understanding of the other side's perspective, explain why that position seems unfair to you.

- **Draw on external criteria and commonsense measures that lend legitimacy to your position.** For example, "Your price of $2,000 per square foot of first-floor retail space in the downtown business district seems excessive. I know, for instance, that three similar spaces within two blocks of your location have recently been leased for less than $1,700 per square foot."

- **Signal your interest in closing the deal.** Let the other party know when you are close to an acceptable deal so that it won't expect many more concessions.

Steps for Closing a Deal

1. **Signal the end of the road before you get there.** As you approach what you would like to be a final deal, say so. Repeat the warning, not as a threat but as a courtesy, particularly if the other negotiator seems to expect much more movement.

2. **Allow flexibility if you anticipate going beyond the final round.** If you are aware that the other negotiator does not have final authority, leave yourself some flexibility, or wiggle room, in the final terms. But don't create so much flexibility that the deal will be rejected by the decision maker. Consider a final trade you would be willing to make if you end up requesting significant adjustment in the final terms.

3. **Discourage the other side from seeking further concessions.**
   If you appear to have reached a final deal that is acceptable to
   the other side (and perhaps also favorable to you), discourage
   further tweaking.
   - Express your willingness to accept the total package, without
     changes.
   - Explain that adjustment in the other party's favor on one term
     would have to be balanced by adjustment in your favor on another.
     For example, you might say, "If we open that issue, then I'm afraid
     we'll have to reopen the whole deal for it to work for me."

4. **Write down the terms.** If your negotiation time has been well
   spent, don't risk ruining it by failing to record and sign your agreement. People's memories of their agreement will inevitably diverge;
   recording the terms of the agreement avoids future disputes and
   confusion.
   - Even if counsel will draft the official documents, write an infor-
     mal agreement in principle. Decide whether or not it is binding,
     and say so in the document.
   - Even if your informal agreement is nonbinding, it will be a com-
     mon text for reference by both parties as future, good-faith
     questions arise.

5. **Don't gloat.** If you brag about your great deal and how much more
   you would have been willing to give up, it will encourage the other
   side to find a way to get it back. It will also increase its aggressiveness in the next negotiation and will increase the aggressiveness of
   anyone who hears the story and later negotiates with you.

Tactics for integrative negotiations

Integrative negotiations rely on collaboration and information exchange to create and claim value. Consider using the following tactics:

- **Don't make a proposal too quickly.** A premature offer won't benefit from information gleaned from the negotiating process. If you are the buyer, such information could, for example, alert you to other potentially beneficial items or terms that you might include in a proposal.

- **Inquire about the other side's interests.** Ask what the other party's needs, interests, and concerns are, and determine the party's willingness to trade off one thing for another. Listen carefully, because the responses can reveal valuable information. Be forthright about your own needs, interests, and concerns.

- **Provide significant information about your circumstances.** Explain why you want to make a deal. Talk about your real interests, preferences among issues or options, and business constraints. Reveal any additional capabilities or resources you have that could be added to the deal.

- **Look for differences to create value.** When you and the other party understand each other's needs and interests, it's more likely that you'll be able to reach a mutually satisfying outcome. Sometimes such an outcome can be carved from the differences between you. By trading on differences, you create value that neither of you could have created on your own.

For example, consider Martha, who owns both a retail store and a restaurant. She is negotiating with Allen, an interior designer, about renovating her restaurant. Martha agrees to pay a somewhat higher price than planned for the restaurant design; in exchange, Allen will order fixtures and furnishings for the retail store at his trade discount. Martha would not otherwise have ready access to these discounts, and yet providing them costs Allen nothing. Value has been created for both sides.

- **Take your time.** Don't be tempted to close the deal too quickly, especially when the first acceptable proposal is on the table but little information has been exchanged. Spend more time finding a deal that is better for both sides. Signal that the proposal on the table is worth considering, but also state that it may be improved by learning more about your respective interests and concerns.

- **Generate options that offer mutual gain.** In preparing for the negotiation, you formulated positions that satisfied your own interests. You are now confronted with the other side's positions. The challenge now: to arrive at an outcome that satisfies both parties' interests. Here are some suggestions for generating win-win solutions:

  - Move from a particular issue to a more general description of the problem, then to theoretical solutions, and finally back to the specific issue.
  - Pay special attention to shared interests and opportunities for cooperation.

- Consider joint brainstorming with the other side; it can be a fruitful way of generating creative alternatives. Set ground rules that encourage participants to express any and all ideas, no matter how wild or impractical. Be careful not to criticize or express disapproval of any suggestion; at this stage, such judgment inhibits creativity, making people reluctant to offer further suggestions—and more likely to criticize any ideas you volunteer as well.

Tips for Listening Actively

You'll learn more about the other side's interests and about opportunities for mutual gain if you practice active listening. Here are some active listening tips:

- Keep your eyes on the speaker.
- Take notes as appropriate.
- Don't allow yourself to think about anything except what the speaker is saying.
- Resist the urge to formulate your response until after the speaker has finished.
- Pay attention to the speaker's body language.
- Ask questions to get more information and to encourage the speaker to continue.
- Repeat in your own words what you've heard to ensure that you understand and to let the speaker know you've processed what you've heard.

Framing the solution

Framing, or how you choose to describe a situation, is useful in both distributive and integrative negotiations. A frame can determine how negotiations will ensue. It orients the parties and encourages them to examine the issues within a defined perspective. How one side frames a solution can determine how others decide to behave. Generally, you can use one of these frames:

- **Present your proposal in terms that represent a gain instead of a loss.** Instead of saying, "My current offer is only 10 percent less than what you are asking," say, "I've already increased my offer by 10 percent."

- **Use risk aversion to your advantage.** Risk-averse people tend to prefer the certainty of a smaller offer to the uncertainty of a larger future gain. For example, you might say, "I know you want $400,000 for that property, and you may get it someday. However, I'm willing to pay $350,000 for it today. Can we make a deal?"

Continual evaluation

Many managers think of negotiation as a linear process of preparation, negotiation, and eventual agreement or failure. But some negotiations are complex and require succeeding rounds. New information may appear at various points, or different parties may offer concessions or heighten their demands.

Complex negotiations often require a nonlinear approach. Preparation is followed by negotiation, which produces outcomes and

Rounds of negotiation

information that require evaluation. The outputs of evaluation then lead to a new round of preparation and subsequent negotiation. This process continues until the parties reach an agreement or walk away from the negotiation.

In this situation, it's important to integrate the new knowledge and circumstances into your strategy and readjust your course as you proceed.

Barriers to
Agreement

MOST CONFLICTS CAN be negotiated successfully if the parties can remain objective and if they aren't driven by pride, impatience, stubbornness, or ignorance of the facts. Many barriers to successful negotiations can be overcome or eliminated if you know how to manage them. Here are some typical barriers to agreement, along with suggestions for dealing with them.

Die-hard bargainers

They are out there—the *die-hard bargainers*, for whom every deal is a battle. How can you work with such highly competitive negotiators? Here are some suggestions:

- **Know their game.** Don't let die-hard bargainers intimidate you. Anticipate unreasonable offers, grudging concessions, and posturing. Don't let this behavior prevent you from analyzing and improving your BATNA. Set your reservation price as well as assess theirs.

- **Be guarded in the information you disclose.** Disclose only the information that cannot be used against you.

- **Suggest alternative packages or options when they are unwilling to share information.** When you present options and packages, the other side tends to ask questions to clarify and compare the offers. Doing so may reveal information that can help you better understand the other side's interests and concerns.

- **Indicate your willingness to walk away.** If the other party sees that its difficult behavior may result in your walking away, it may back down and become more cooperative.

Lack of trust

You suspect that the other side is lying or bluffing. It may have no intention of following through on its promises. How should you respond?

- **Emphasize the need for integrity.** Stress that a deal is predicated on its accurate and truthful representations.

- **Request documentation.** Insist on documentation, and make the terms of the deal contingent on the accuracy of that documentation.

- **Insist on enforcement mechanisms.** Add contingencies to the deal, such as a security deposit, an escrow arrangement, or penalties for noncompliance (or perhaps positive incentives for early performance).

Potential saboteurs

Whenever people perceive themselves as losers in the outcome of a negotiation, expect resistance and possible sabotage. Stakeholders, employees, and customers can all be potential saboteurs if they have the power to block your negotiations.

Resistance may be passive, in the form of noncommitment to the goals and the process for reaching them, or active, in the form of direct opposition or subversion. Particularly in multiparty negotiations, certain stakeholders may prefer "no deal" to the outcome. Anticipate and prepare for this possibility.

Tips for Dealing with Saboteurs

- **Identify potential saboteurs.** Map out the stakeholders, their respective interests, and their power to affect the agreement and its implementation.
- **Consider augmenting the deal.** Include something in the deal to benefit stakeholders who would otherwise have the incentive to sabotage.
- **Communicate potential benefits to resisters.** Those benefits might be greater future job security, higher pay, and so on. There's no guarantee that the benefits will exceed the losses to these individuals, but explaining the benefits will help shift their focus from negatives to positives.
- **Help resisters find new roles.** Those new roles should represent genuine contributions and mitigate their losses.
- **Think about the issue of control.** Some people resist change because it represents a loss of control over their lives. You can return some of that control by making them active partners in the negotiation process or in your change program.
- **Build a coalition with sufficient strength to overpower the saboteurs.** A coalition may shift the balance of negotiating power in your favor.

Differences in gender and culture

People often attribute a breakdown in negotiation to gender or cultural differences, but these may not be the cause of the problem. For example, you might think, "The problem is that she's a woman and can't deal with confrontation." Or, "He's late because that's how Italians are with time." When you attribute these problems to gender or culture, you may miss the true issue: the female negotiator is signaling her company's resistance point, or there are efficiency and production problems at the Italian company.

If you are having difficulty understanding or working with someone from another culture or the opposite gender, consider these guidelines:

- **Look for a pattern to diagnose the problem.** What kinds of issues create difficulties? What types of misunderstandings have you had?

- **Consider what assumptions each party has brought to the table.** Are they valid? Are any related specifically to the negotiation at hand or to the particular company, and not to differences in culture?

- **Research possible areas of difference.** Review any available literature about the other party's culture and how it compares with yours.

- **Use what you've learned to establish more comfortable communication.** Adjust your communication style, or articulate the differing norms or assumptions you believe to have been the source of the problem.

Communication problems

Communication is the medium of negotiation. You cannot make progress without it. When you suspect that a negotiation is disintegrating because of communication problems, try the following steps:

- **Ask for a break.** Take some time to clear your head, refocus, and regain objectivity.

- **Look for a pattern.** Mentally replay what has been communicated, how, and by whom. Does the confusion or misunderstanding arise from a single issue? Did you have assumptions or expectations that were not articulated? Did the other side?

- **After the break, raise the issue in a nonaccusatory way.** Offer to listen while the other side explains its perspective on the issue. Listen actively, acknowledging the other point of view. Explain your perspective. Then try to pinpoint the problem.

- **Switch spokespeople.** If the spokesperson for your negotiating team seems to frustrate the other side, have someone else act in this role. Ask the other team to do the same if its representative irritates your party.

- **Jointly document progress as it is made.** This is particularly important in multiphase negotiations. It will solve the problem of someone saying, "I don't remember agreeing to that."

Cognitive
Traps

U NFORTUNATELY, EVEN THE most even-tempered and objective people fall prey to cognitive errors as they negotiate. This section describes some of those mental errors and explains how you can avoid and correct them.

Irrational escalation

Irrational escalation occurs when commitment or conflict intensifies or expands in ways that make little sense. Some negotiators make this error when they cannot stand the thought of losing. Others get caught up in "auction fever," irrational behavior that surfaces when auctions and other bidding contests pit individuals against each other. To avoid irrational escalation, keep these tips in mind:

- **Know your BATNA before you negotiate.** Remind yourself that money you don't throw away on an overpriced deal is money you'll have available to invest in your other alternatives.

- **Before negotiations, work with your team to set a reasonable reservation price.** If the entire team decides on a number, you'll be less tempted to escalate your price during negotiation. If new information arises, objectively recalculate your reservation price with your team.

- **Set clear breakpoints.** During the negotiation, periodically stop and assess your situation to ensure you are not getting off track.

Partisan perception

Partisan perception is the psychological phenomenon that causes people to perceive "truth" with a built-in bias toward their own point of view. For example, loyal fans of a team may perceive an umpire's ruling as unfair to their side. To avoid partisan perception, recognize it as a phenomenon, and remember these guidelines:

- **Try to see the issue from the perspective of the other party.** This will help you see the other side's partisan viewpoints.

- **Pose the issue to colleagues.** Explain the situation, and solicit their opinions without telling them which side you are on.

- **Carefully frame the problem.** When conveying your position to the other party, pose the problem as it appears to you, and ask how they view it.

- **Involve a neutral third party.** Suggest bringing in a neutral third party or expert to provide unbiased guidance.

Unreasonable expectations

Some people enter negotiations with unreasonable expectations and, as a result, eliminate any zone of possible agreement. For example, consider a first-time author who submits her book proposal to a publisher. The publisher likes her proposal but won't agree to

What Would YOU Do?

Are You Using All Your Options?

C LAUDIA IS PART OF A team negotiating a licensing
agreement between her software company and SPX Systems, a computer hardware manufacturer. Over the past several months Claudia's team has negotiated similar agreements on very favorable terms. "And why not?" she tells herself. "Our software is remarkable. We are the best in the business. SPX should agree to our terms." Her teammates agree and are willing to play hardball. But SPX's negotiators aren't rolling over, and talks appear to be falling apart.

What would you do in this situation?

---

her demand of a $100,000 advance. Instead, the publisher offers her $10,000. With the publisher's reservation price of $10,000 and the author's of $100,000, there is no overlap in which an agreement can be struck and the negotiations fall apart. To avoid this situation, remember these tips:

- **Explain the rationale behind your thinking.** If the other party presents unrealistic expectations, explain *why* these demands are not reasonable. For example, the publisher could have talked with the author about the number of copies that would need to be sold to earn $100,000 in royalties, and he could explain how past sales of similar books have never attained those figures. This explanation might have induced the author to reduce her reservation price.

- **Provide new information.** If you believe that the other party should increase its reservation price, provide factual information in support of your view. For example, if the author had a letter from someone who had already committed to purchasing a large number of copies of her book, it might have helped change the publisher's expectation of future sales—and his reservation price.

- **Make sure your expectations are realistic.** To avoid forming unrealistic expectations, take a look at similar situations. These will help you bring your expectations in line with reality.

Overconfidence

Confidence is an important attribute during negotiations. It provides the courage you need to tackle difficult and uncertain ventures. Too much confidence, however, can set negotiators up for failure. It encourages them to overestimate their strengths and underestimate their rivals, and it makes them blind to dangers.

Unchecked emotions

People sometimes assume that emotion and irrationality occur in personal negotiations, but rarely in business. This is not so. Some people become angry and emotional in difficult commercial transactions. When emotion takes control of a negotiation, the parties often stop focusing on logical and rational solutions, and the dialogue falls apart. To overcome unchecked emotion and irrationality, use the following strategies:

- **Suggest a cooling-off period.** Call for a break in negotiations. Some distance from the discussion can calm high-strung emotions and restore objectivity.

- **Determine what is making the other party angry.** Try to understand what this deal or dispute means to the other party. Listen carefully to its comments, and try to determine what is fueling the anger.

- **Be responsive.** Once you understand what is making the other party angry, express empathy.

- **Focus on the issues, not on opposing negotiators.** People can lose their focus when they feel personally attacked, deceived, humiliated, or disrespected. So keep discussions impersonal and focused on the issues.

- **Enlist an objective moderator.** If you cannot make progress with the other party because of high emotions, suggest bringing in a neutral facilitator.

What You COULD Do.

Step Back, Rethink.

Claudia and her teammates may have a case of overconfidence—a malady that could forestall a potentially profitable relationship with a new customer. To avoid the perils of overconfident actions and decisions, Claudia and her teammates should try to put a little psychological distance between themselves and their situation and, from that perspective, reexamine the positions and interests of both sides. For example, they might ask, "Our software might be terrific, but is it the best from the perspective of SPX's intended use?" Alternatively, they might ask one or more objective outsiders to examine their key assumptions, the position of the other party, and the deal on the table.

The Skills of Effective Negotiators

The most important trip you may ever take
in life is meeting people half way.
—Henry Boyle

W HAT MAKES AN EFFECTIVE negotiator? Many of the skills and methods that talented negotiators use are developed over time with lots of practice. With training and experience, you can develop and strengthen your negotiating skills, too. To increase your effectiveness, focus on the following skills:

- **Align negotiating goals with organizational goals.** Effective negotiators operate within a framework that supports the strategic goals of their organization.

- **Be thoroughly prepared.** An effective negotiator collects as much information as possible in advance of deliberations, is organized for all meetings, and uses each negotiating phase to prepare for the next.

- **Determine the other side's BATNA and reservation price.** An astute negotiator uses dialog with the other party and away-from-the-table detective work to ascertain the other side's BATNA and reservation price.

- **Identify the interests of both sides, and develop value-creating options.** A sharp negotiator can help the other side see the value of sharing information and expanding value opportunities.

- **Separate personal issues from negotiating issues.** Accomplished negotiators know that the issues being discussed are not about them—or even about the individuals sitting across the table. Instead, accomplished negotiators operate with objective detachment and focus on producing the best possible outcome.

- **Recognize potential barriers to agreement.** Barriers aren't always obvious. A skillful negotiator finds and neutralizes them.

- **Know how to form coalitions.** Not every negotiator is dealt a winning hand. The other side often has greater power. A good negotiator, however, knows that a coalition of several weak players can often counter that power. More important, a skilled negotiator knows how to build such a coalition on a foundation of shared interests.

- **Develop a reputation for reliability and trustworthiness.** The most effective negotiations are built on trust. Trust formed through one phase of negotiation pays dividends in the next. A negotiator earns trust by practicing ethical behavior and by following through on all promises.

- **Recognize relationship value.** Some negotiations, usually the integrative type, involve parties that have important

Tips for Managing Relationship Value

- **Create trust.** Trust is created when people see tangible evidence that your words and actions are in harmony. So avoid making commitments you may not be able to honor, and always do what you have committed to do. Trust is also created when you acknowledge and demonstrate respect for the other party's core interests.
- **Communicate.** Negotiating parties should communicate their interests, capabilities, and concerns to each other. For example, if you've committed to finishing a project for a client by a certain date but you then run into scheduling conflicts that will make your project late, communicate that information to your client immediately.
- **Never try to hide mistakes.** Mistakes are bound to happen. Acknowledging and addressing them—quickly—is always the best course of action.
- **Ask for feedback.** If everything appears to be going as planned, don't assume that the other side sees it the same way. Be proactive in uncovering problems. The other side will respect you for it. Ask questions such as these: "Is everything happening as you expected?" "Are the parts reaching your plant on schedule?" "Did my report cover all the important points?"

relationships they hope to retain. For example, managers want to maintain positive relationships with their direct subordinates, manufacturers want to preserve strong relations with their key suppliers, and so on. An effective negotiator recognizes the importance of long-term relationships and knows how to retain them by creating trust, communicating openly, admitting to and addressing mistakes, and asking for feedback.

Tips and Tools

Tools for
Negotiating Outcomes

Determining Your Reservation Price

Use this worksheet to examine the variables that can determine your reservation price.

1. Explore the variables that affect your reservation, or "walk-away," position.

What is the value to you of the deal on the table?

How does this compare to the value of your BATNA?

What other values need to be considered?

If there is a dollar number involved in the negotiation, what is the lowest amount that you would consider?

What are the minimum nondollar terms that you would consider?

2. Evaluate the trade-offs between your issues and interests.

Which issues or terms do you care most about?

Are any of these issues or terms linked? *(That is, does more or less of what you want on one issue give you more or less flexibility on any of the others?)*

How much of what you want on one issue or term would you trade off against another?

Are there different package deals that would be equivalent in value to you?

3. Articulate the parameters of your reservation price. *(The resulting terms or price create the context for you to evaluate alternative proposals.)*

Assessing the Other Side's Interests

Use this worksheet to summarize your knowledge of the other side's interests. Refer to this information throughout the negotiation process, and use it to identify value-creating opportunities.

Learn about the other side.	Yes	No
1. Have you spoken with people—either formally or informally—who know the other party?		
2. Have you reviewed the other side's Web site, marketing materials, and (if applicable) annual reports and public findings?		
3. Have you researched the other side's industry and contacted sources within the industry to find out more?		
4. Have you imagined what the other side's interests, preferences, and needs would be if you were in its position?		

Assess the other side's BATNA.

What do you know about the other side's business circumstances?
How strong is its financial performance?

What is its strategy?

What are its key corporate initiatives?

What competitive pressures does it face?

What do you know about the value this deal has to the other side?
How important is this deal to the other side at this time?

Is it necessary for the other side to meet a larger objective? *(Describe the objective.)*

What do you know about the availability of a replacement deal?
Is your offer easy to find elsewhere?

Can it be obtained in time to meet the other side's deadlines?

Has the other side already obtained bids from or initiated informal negotiations with anyone else?

Consider the terms the other side would like to see for the deal.

What broader business objectives would the other side like to see served by this deal?

What terms of this deal could hamper its business growth?

What terms might you offer that would benefit the other side (at a low cost to you)?

Identifying and Improving Your BATNA

*Use this worksheet to identify and improve your best alternative
to a negotiated agreement, or BATNA.*

1. What are your alternatives to a negotiated agreement?
Make a list of what your alternatives will be if the negotiation ends without agreement.

1.

2.

3.

4.

5.

2. Of the alternatives that you listed, which is your best alternative?

3. Can you improve your BATNA?

Are there any arrangements you can make with other suppliers, partners, or customers that would improve your BATNA?

Are there ways to remove or alter any constraints that currently weaken your BATNA? If yes, what? How?

Are there ways to change your terms of the negotiation to improve your BATNA? If yes, what? How?

4. What will your new BATNA be if you succeed in improving it?

Evaluating Your Authority and That of the Other Side

Use this worksheet to determine and confirm the authority level you have and the authority level of the persons with whom you will be negotiating, so that you can plan accordingly.

The other side's authority. *(Learn as much as possible about the individuals on the other side.)*

1. Who will be at the negotiating table?

2. What are the formal titles and areas of responsibility of the persons with whom you will be negotiating?

3. How long have they been with the company? What other relevant experience do they have?

4. How is the company structured? *(Is it hierarchical, with significant decision-making powers centered at the top, or is it relatively decentralized?)*

5. How are the negotiators viewed within the organization? *(Are they generally respected, listened to, etc.? Rely on contacts outside the organization, if available.)*

6. What are their other interests outside work (e.g., sports, hobbies, volunteer interests, political orientation, children)?

Your authority. *(Confirm in as much detail as possible.)*

What kind of deal are you authorized to make? (Complete as appropriate.)

Only a predetermined deal for which committee approval has been obtained? *(If yes, describe. If you can also negotiate something "better" beyond the predetermined deal, what does the committee consider "better"?)*

Only a deal that meets certain objectives? *(What are the objectives? Do you have the freedom to structure the deal in the best way you can?)*

Would the committee prefer that you bring a deal back for formal review and approval?

Is your authority limited on monetary issues but not on other creative options without significant financial implications?

Are you authorized to provide information about your company's needs, interests, and preferences if the other side engages in a good-faith, reciprocal exchange?

Sales Negotiation Planning Form

Use this sales planning form to prepare for an upcoming sales negotiation.

Account:
   Date:

1. Define issues the account may want to negotiate and why *(such as price, volume discount, extended terms).*

Issue/Why	Underlying account need, perceived or real

2. Describe each competitor's advantages and disadvantages compared to your product or service.

Competitor name(s)	Competitor's advantages *(product features, services, marketing, pricing, etc.)*	Competitor's disadvantages *(potential weak spots)*

3. For each key issue, think through what you will give and what you will ask for in return.

Issue	What you will give	What you will ask for

4. Prepare your position and offer range.

What is your offer and your rationale for it?

How might the account react to this offer? How would you handle that?

What's your reservation price or walk-away position (or least favorable offer you will accept)?

If the other side fails to meet your reservation price, what other areas of possible agreement can you explore?

Test Yourself

This section offers ten multiple-choice questions to help you see what you've learned and identify areas that you might want to explore further. The answers are found at the end of this section.

1. What is a distributive negotiation?

   a. A type of negotiation in which the parties compete for the distribution of a fixed pool of value, and any gain by one party represents a loss to the other

   b. A type of negotiation in which the parties cooperate to achieve maximum mutual benefit in an agreement

   c. A type of negotiation that involves more than two parties

2. Which of the following would be an example of an integrative negotiation?

   a. The sale of a car

   b. A wage negotiation between a business owner and a union of employees

   c. The structuring of a long-term partnership for a corporation

3. You are seeking to purchase a new home and have set a reservation price of $300,000. The seller of the home you are interested in has a reservation price of $325,000. What is the ZOPA (zone of possible agreement)?

   a. There is no ZOPA in this example.

   b. $300,000 to $325,000

   c. Any number less than $300,000

4. Why is it important to know your BATNA before walking into a negotiation?

   a. Your BATNA enables you to create value through trades.

   b. Your BATNA determines the point at which you can say no to an unfavorable proposal.

   c. Your BATNA helps you identify when it is advantageous to form a coalition.

5. In which type of negotiation should you reveal information about your interests, preferences, and business constraints?

   a. You should never reveal information about your circumstances.

   b. Distributive negotiations

   c. Integrative negotiations

6. What strategy should you implement if you don't trust the other party?

    a. Identify potential saboteurs.

    b. Suggest alternative packages or options.

    c. Insist on enforcement mechanisms.

7. Which of the following is a strategy you can use to avoid partisan perceptions?

    a. Imagine yourself in the other side's position.

    b. Before negotiations, work with your team to set a reasonable reservation price.

    c. Set clear breakpoints.

8. In negotiations, what is an anchor?

    a. An anchor is the first offer that is made.

    b. An anchor is a complex deal that requires a nonlinear approach to negotiating.

    c. An anchor is the way you choose to describe a negotiation.

9. What is the first step you should take in preparing for a negotiation?

    a. Identify your BATNA.

    b. Determine satisfactory outcomes.

    c. Study the other side.

10. How should you react when the other side opens the negotiation with an unreasonable offer?

    a. Ask questions that make the other negotiator justify the offer.

    b. Counter with a similarly unreasonable offer to put the other side on the defensive.

    c. Get up from the table and begin to leave the room so that the other party changes the offer.

Answers to test questions

1, a. A type of negotiation in which the parties compete for the distribution of a fixed pool of value, and any gain by one party represents a loss to the other.

    A distributive negotiation is also sometimes referred to as a zero-sum or win-lose negotiation because a gain by one side is made at the expense of the other.

2, c. The structuring of a long-term partnership for a corporation.

    In this case, the parties work cooperatively to make trade-offs so that everyone walks out of the deal feeling satisfied. The relationship between the parties is valued.

3, a. There is no ZOPA in this example.

    In this situation, there is no overlap between the ranges that you and the seller find acceptable. No agreement would be possible, no matter how skilled you both were, unless there were other elements of value to be considered—or one or both of you changed your reservation price.

4, b. Your BATNA determines the point at which you can say no to an unfavorable proposal.

BATNA—or best alternative to a negotiated agreement—is your preferred course of action if you cannot reach agreement in the negotiation at hand. Your BATNA determines the point at which you can say no to an unfavorable proposal. If your BATNA is good, you can afford to negotiate for more favorable terms.

5, c. Integrative negotiations.

Integrative negotiations rely on collaboration and information exchange to create and claim value, so it's important to reveal information about your circumstances in this type of negotiation.

6, c. Insist on enforcement mechanisms.

If you don't fully trust the other party, it's prudent to add contingencies—such as a security deposit, escrow arrangement, or penalties for noncompliance or perhaps positive incentives for early performance—into the deal.

7, a Imagine yourself in the other side's position.

Try to view the negotiation from the perspective of the other party's negotiators. This will help you see their partisan viewpoints.

8, a. An anchor is the first offer that is made.

The anchor sets the bargaining range. Studies show that negotiation outcomes often correlate to the first offer, so it's important to start negotiations at the right place. It's best to anchor when you have a strong sense of the other side's reservation price, and your proposal should be at or just a bit higher than that number.

9, b. Determine satisfactory outcomes.

A negotiation's success is determined by its outcome; therefore, it's best to be clear about what constitutes a good outcome for you and the other side before the negotiation begins. Satisfactory outcomes typically address the interests—underlying motivations, needs, and concerns—of each party.

10, a. Move to another specific topic, and then explain your perspective on the deal and make your offer. Or, if the apparently unreasonable offer seems to have been put forth seriously, ask questions that make the other negotiator justify the offer.

Clearly state that the offer is entirely out of the range you had imagined, and then ask such questions as, "How did you arrive at that number?" "What is it based on?" "How can I justify this number to my company?"

Frequently Asked Questions

When asked by the other side to name a dollar figure, is it OK to state my range?

Do not state your range unless you will be happy with a deal that is at the least favorable end of that range. For example, if you tell someone that you would pay $20,000 to $25,000 for a piece of property, rest assured that you will pay at least $25,000.

The only reason to mention a range is to discourage the other side from pushing you beyond it, and this should happen toward the end of the negotiating process. For example, if after several rounds of back-and-forth on a dollar figure, you are at $23,000 and the other side is at $30,000 and seems to be pushing for $28,000, you could say, "My preferred range walking into this negotiation was $20,000 to $23,000, but not above $25,000." The seller may be able to accept $25,000 more easily because he will feel he has pushed you over the top of your range.

Is it smart or fair to bluff?

It's OK to bluff, but it's not OK to lie. Lying about a material fact in a negotiation is unethical and is almost certainly grounds for legal action. In certain circumstances, creating a false impression or failing to disclose material information may be a formal ethical breach and actionable as well.

As long as what you bring to the table has real value, you need not reveal all the circumstances making you desperate for a deal. Thus, if you are negotiating the terms of a job offer, there is nothing wrong with describing the major projects for which you have been responsible, and the likely next step on the corporate ladder in your current company. You need not mention that the new division president is impossible to deal with or that one or two projects have not turned out well. This is not hard bargaining; it is effective self-advocacy or salesmanship.

Should I ever tell the other side my real bottom line?

The only time it makes sense to tell the other side your real bottom line is when you've reached it or are about to reach it. If you do reveal your bottom line, make sure you call it just that, with appropriate emphasis or firmness. Otherwise, the other side may not take you seriously and may view that number as just another step on the way to a final deal.

In a complex deal, is it better to reach agreement issue by issue, or wait until the end?

Every deal is unique, but generally it's better to discuss packages of terms or options. Then aim for tentative agreements or agreed-upon ranges as you work through each issue or linked groups of issues. This approach gives you the necessary flexibility to make value-creating trade-offs between issues and to create alternative packages of options.

Which is it better to deal with first—difficult issues or easy issues?

In general, dealing with easier issues first helps build momentum, deepens the parties' commitment to the process, and enables the parties to become familiar with each other before discussing the tough issues. In some instances, however, you may want to begin with a more difficult issue. If you cannot reach tentative agreement on the difficult issues, then you will not have wasted time on the smaller ones. It is also true that once the most difficult issue is resolved, smaller issues often fall into place more easily.

How should I respond if the other side seeks to change something after a deal has been reached?

Chances are that whenever a deal is reached, one or both of the parties become cursed with the thought that it could have gotten more. If the other side seeks to change one item, express surprise or disappointment. Explain that if it makes a change, then it must understand that you will want to open up other issues as well. You agreed to a total package, and one change affects that package. If the other side agrees to renegotiate other issues, then it is probably sincere, and you should proceed with the renegotiation. If it reconsiders and withdraws the request for change, then it was just testing you. If the other side insists that it must have this change and no others, you can express dismay, but you must decide whether the adjusted deal has sufficient value for you to agree.

What should I do when the negotiator on the other side has an emotional outburst?

Your counterpart must be rational and in control of his emotions. Don't respond in kind; instead, try to help him regain control.

- Sit quietly. After he has stopped shouting, ask whether there is anything you have done to make him angry. Listen calmly and actively. Resume negotiations with a calm voice.

- If the other party's outburst persists, get up and turn to leave the room. As you get to the door, calmly explain that you understand that something has made him angry, but you can't continue to negotiate if such an outburst might occur again. Suggest that he calm down. You might also say that you need time to calm down after hearing his outburst. Suggest that he call you in a day or two if he wants to continue the negotiation.

If his shouting was intended to get you upset, don't reward that strategy. Think seriously about walking away from the deal. Dealing with this person in the future may not be worth the headache. Depending on the situation, you might contact someone else in the company to suggest that another negotiator be assigned to the deal.

Is it essential to negotiate face-to-face?

If the negotiation concerns a simple issue, where personal communication is not likely to matter, face-to-face negotiations are not necessary. If the deal is more complicated or if you sense that the other side may be tempted to lie, it is better to negotiate face-to-face. Some research indicates that people are less likely to lie in person, perhaps because they fear that the other side will detect it. When you are in a face-to-face negotiation, you're likely to pick up the nonverbal cues that indicate something is amiss. On the phone, you may be able to interpret tone of voice; however, some recent research indicates that people are more likely to bluff in this situation.

E-mail or other written messages occasionally result in disputes and impasses. The person who receives a written message may interpret a comment negatively when the sender did not intend it that way, and may respond to the original sender in kind.

How should I react when the other side opens with a very unreasonable number?

Don't counter with an equally unreasonable number; doing so will make the negotiation still more difficult. Instead, state that the offer is entirely out of the range you had anticipated. Then use one of these strategies:

- Change the subject by asking about a specific issue. Explain your perspective on the deal and its value. After some discussion, suggest a number you can justify as reasonable, and that is in the favorable end of your range or close to the other side's reservation price, whichever is better. Do *not* refer to the initial number or proposal.

- If the apparently unreasonable offer appears to have been serious, ask questions to understand it and to make the negotiator justify the offer. For example, ask, "How did you arrive at that number?" "What is it based on?" "How can I justify this number to my company?" The danger of this strategy is that it may lock the other negotiator into that initial number and make subsequent sizable concessions more difficult.

Key Terms

BATNA. The acronym for "best alternative to a negotiated agreement." Knowing your BATNA means knowing the options of what you will do or what will happen if you do not reach agreement in the negotiation at hand. For example, the BATNA for a consultant negotiating with a potential client about a monthlong assignment might be to spend three weeks developing marketing materials for a different client.

Bluffing. When one party in a negotiation indicates that it may be willing to do or accept something that it actually has no intention of following through on. For example, a tenant may bluff that he will not renew his lease unless certain improvements are made to his office space.

Die-hard bargainers. People for whom every negotiation is a battle.

Distributive negotiation (zero-sum negotiation). One of two types of negotiation, this type occurs when the parties compete over the distribution of the benefits of an agreement. In the sale of a house, for example, each party wants the best for itself at the expense of the other.

Framing.   How one chooses to describe a situation. Framing orients negotiating parties and encourages them to examine the issues within a defined perspective. How one side frames a solution can determine how others decide to behave.

Integrative negotiation (win-win negotiation).   One of two types of negotiation, this type occurs when the parties cooperate to achieve maximum mutual benefit in an agreement. Long-term partnerships and collaborations between colleagues are often characterized by integrative negotiation.

Interests.   The goals underlying a party's negotiation position.

Irrational escalation.   The continuation of a selected course of action beyond the point where it continues to make sense.

Multiparty negotiations.   Negotiations that involve more than two parties. Such negotiations can differ significantly from two-party negotiations, especially when coalitions—alliances among parties that wield less power separately than they do together—form among the parties.

Multiphase transactions.   Negotiations that are implemented in phases, or that have the prospect of subsequent involvement in the future. The context of the negotiations allows parties to negotiate based on follow-through and continuing communication.

Natural coalition.   A group of allies that share a broad range of common interests.

Negotiator's dilemma.   The tension caused by a negotiator's attempt to balance competitive strategies—trying to discern when to compete where interests conflict, and when to create value by exchanging the information that leads to mutually advantageous options.

Partisan perception.   The psychological phenomenon that causes people to perceive truth with a built-in bias in their own favor or toward their own point of view. For example, both teams in a football game may perceive that the referee was unfair to their side.

Positions.   What the parties in a negotiation are asking for—in other words, their demands.

Reservation price (walk-away).   The least favorable point at which a party would accept a negotiated deal. The reservation price is derived from, but is not usually the same thing as, a BATNA.

Saboteurs.   Internal or external stakeholders who have the power or intention (or both) of blocking a deal.

Shared interests.   Part of an integrative, or win-win, strategy, this tactic involves appealing to interests or goals that are shared by both parties in a negotiation.

Single-issue coalition. A group whose members may differ on other issues but who nevertheless unite (often for different reasons) to support or block a particular issue.

Strategy. A planned sequence of how one will approach a negotiation, including what the negotiator will offer and ask for (give and get).

Tactics. The specific methods for implementing a strategy.

Trade off. To substitute or bargain one issue for another; this tactic is often used in sales negotiations.

Value creation through trades. The trading of goods or services that have only modest value to their holders but exceptional value to the other party.

ZOPA. The acronym for the "zone of possible agreement." This is the area in which a potential deal can take place. Each party's reservation price defines one of the boundaries of the ZOPA. The ZOPA itself exists, if at all, in the overlap between the parties' reservation prices.

To Learn More

Articles

Field, Anne. "How to Negotiate with a Hard-Nosed Adversary." *Harvard Management Update* (March 2003).

If you go into a negotiation expecting to meet a tough opponent, you just might get one. But with careful preparation and the right game plan, you can turn the tables on an aggressive opponent. Don't take your opponent's tough guy reputation at face value. Consider reducing the time you have to spend with the tough adversary, plan your comebacks ahead of time, research all the options you have, and then, finally, identify your BATNA (best alternative to a negotiated agreement). By taking this advice to heart, you'll be surprised by how easy your next negotiation will be, even if your adversary has a tough reputation.

Galinsky, Adam D. "Should You Make the First Offer?" *Negotiation* (July 2004).

Whether negotiators are bidding on a firm, seeking agreement on a compensation package, or bargaining over a used car, someone has to make the first offer. Should it be you, or should you wait to hear what others have to say? How will the first offer influence the negotiation process and any final agreement? New research on the anchoring effect suggests that the best strategy is often to speak up first.

Lax, David A., and James K. Sebenius. "3-D Negotiation: Playing the Whole Game." *Harvard Business Review* OnPoint Enhanced Edition (2003).

What stands between you and the yes you want? According to these negotiation experts, executives face obstacles in three common and complementary dimensions: tactics, or interactions at the bargaining table; deal design, or the ability to draw up a deal at the table that creates lasting value; and setup, which includes the structure of the negotiation itself. Each dimension is crucial in the bargaining process, but most executives fixate on only the first two: 1-D negotiators focus on improving their interpersonal skills at the negotiating table, and 2-D negotiators focus on diagnosing underlying sources of value in a deal and then recrafting the terms to satisfy all parties. In this article, the authors explore the often-neglected third dimension. Instead of just playing the game at the bargaining table, 3-D negotiators reshape the scope and sequence of the game itself to achieve the desired outcome. They scan widely to identify elements outside the deal on the table that might create a more favorable structure for it. They map backward from their ideal resolution to the current setup of the deal and carefully choose which players to approach and when. And they manage and frame the flow of information among the parties involved to improve their odds of getting to yes.

Parker, Susan. "Block That Tactic!" *Harvard Management Communication Letter* (September 2003).

You're putting together a critical business deal when suddenly the client with whom you're negotiating becomes difficult. What do you do? When your negotiation partners aren't playing fair, your best defense is a communication strategy that effectively counters them.

Sander, Frank E. A. "How to Break a Stalemate." *Negotiation* (June 2004).

In any negotiation, parties can come to a stalemate. How do you get out of it? There are two broad strategies that can help you finalize contracts and resolve any conflicts that later ensue: clarifying the other side's needs and interests, and considering other alternatives. Read in-depth advice on how to resolve a negotiating impasse.

Simpson, Liz. "Get Around Resistance and Win Over the Other Side." *Harvard Management Communication Letter* (April 2003).

You're confronting people across the table who have their heels dug in, holding on to a position that is virtually opposite your own. You talk, they talk, but neither of you moves. How can you turn the stalemate into a chance to move the opposition around to your point of view? Read the five tips offered by motivation and persuasion experts to make your attempts in the negotiation game more successful.

Books

Cohen, Steven. *Negotiating Skills for Managers.* New York: McGraw-Hill Trade, 2002.

Virtually everything in business is negotiated, and the ability to negotiate strong agreements and understandings is among today's most valuable talents. *Negotiating Skills for Managers* explains how to establish a solid prenegotiation foundation, subtly guide the negotiation, and consistently set and achieve satisfactory targets. From transferring one's existing strengths to the negotiating table to avoiding common negotiating errors, this book reveals battle-proven steps for reaching personal and organizational objectives in every negotiation.

Fisher, Roger, William Ury, and Bruce Patton. *Getting to Yes: Negotiating Agreement Without Giving In.* 2d ed. New York: Penguin, 1991.

If you read only one book and it must be short, this is it. The original 1981 edition has had a tremendous impact on everything from international politics to professional schools and executive education courses in negotiation. *Getting to Yes* sets up a polemic between "positional bargaining" and "principled negotiation." The heart of the book articulates a basic prescriptive framework for "principled negotiation" or "negotiation on the merits" (separate the people from the problem; focus on interests, not positions; invent options for mutual gain; insist on objective criteria).

Harvard Business School Publishing. *Winning Negotiations That Maintain Relationships: The Results-Driven Manager Series.* Boston: Harvard Business School Press, 2004.

Managers are under increasing pressure to deliver better results faster than the competition. But meeting today's tough challenges requires mastery of a full array of management skills, from communicating and coaching to public speaking and managing people. The Results-Driven Manager series is designed to help time-pressed managers hone and polish the skills they need most. Concise, action oriented, and packed with invaluable strategies and tools, these timely guides help managers improve their job performance today—and give them the edge they need to become the leaders of tomorrow. *Winning Negotiations That Maintain Relationships* urges managers to lead with a compelling argument, deal with difficult adversaries, avoid cross-cultural pitfalls, create formidable alliances, and build strong relationships for future negotiations.

Video

Fisher, Roger, William Ury, and Bruce Patton. *Getting to Yes! Video Workshop on Negotiation.* Videocassette. Boston: Harvard Business School Publishing, 1991.

This video workshop is the next best thing to having Roger Fisher as your managers' personal negotiation trainer and coach. It brings Fisher's work to life and makes it easy to apply to your managers' own situations. You'll see more than a dozen vignettes that vividly illustrate how to turn adversarial negotiations into mutual problem solving. The workshop gives you everything you need to help your managers become more powerful negotiators.

Sources for Negotiating Outcomes

Axelrod, Robert M. *The Evolution of Cooperation.* New York: Basic Books, 1984.

Bazerman, Max H. *Judgment in Managerial Decision Making.* Hoboken, NJ: Wiley Text Books, 2001.

Bazerman, Max H., and Margaret Neale. *Negotiating Rationally.* New York: The Free Press, 1992.

Carlisle, John, and Neil Rackham. "The Behavior of Successful Negotiations." A Report from Huthwaite, Inc. Purcelleville, VA, 1994.

Fisher, Roger, William Ury, and Bruce Patton. *Getting to Yes: Negotiating Agreement Without Giving In.* 2d ed. New York: Penguin, 1991.

Harvard Business School Publishing. *Negotiation.* Boston: Harvard Business School Press, 2004.

Kennedy, Gavin. *Field Guide to Negotiation: A Glossary of Essential Tools and Concepts for Today's Manager.* Boston: Harvard Business/The Economist Reference Series, 1994.

Lax, David, and James K. Sebenius. *The Manager as Negotiator: Bargaining for Cooperation and Competitive Gain.* New York: The Free Press, 1988.

Mnookin, Robert, Scott Peppet, and Andrew Tulumello. "The Tension Between Empathy and Assertiveness." *Negotiation Journal* 12, no. 3 (July 1996).

Rackham, Neil. *SPIN Selling*. New York: McGraw-Hill, 1988.

Raiffa, Howard. *The Art and Science of Negotiation*. Cambridge, MA: Belknap Press of Harvard University Press, 1982.

Rubin, Jeffrey Z., and Frank E.A. Sander. "Culture, Negotiation, and the Eye of the Beholder." *Negotiation Journal* 7, no. 3 (1991).

Sebenius, James K. "The Program on Negotiation for Senior Executives." Executive education program, Program on Negotiation, Harvard Law School.

Shell, Richard. "When Is It Legal to Lie in Negotiations?" *Sloan Management Review* 32, no. 3 (spring 1991).

Valley, Kathleen. "Increasing HR Effectiveness." Executive education program, Program on Negotiation, Harvard Law School.

Notes

Notes

Notes

Notes

Notes

Notes

Notes

Notes

Notes

Notes

Notes

Notes

Notes

How to Order

Harvard Business School Press publications are available world-wide from your local bookseller or online retailer.

You can also call:
1-800-668-6780

Our product consultants are available to help you 8:00 a.m.–6:00 p.m., Monday–Friday, Eastern Time. Outside the U.S. and Canada, call: 617-783-7450.

Please call about special discounts for quantities greater than ten.

You can order online at:
www.HBSPress.org